PowerKids Readers

Brushing My Teeth

Elizabeth Vogel

The Rosen Publishing Group's
PowerKids Press™
New York

1

Published in 2001 by The Rosen Publishing Group, Inc.
29 East 21st Street, New York, NY 10010

First Edition

Book Design: Danielle Primiceri
Layout: Felicity Erwin

Photo Illustrations: Thaddeus Harden

Vogel, Elizabeth.
    Brushing my teeth / by Elizabeth Vogel.
        p. cm.— (PowerKids Readers clean and healthy all day long)
    Includes index.
    Summary: A girl describes how she brushes her teeth and how the process cleans off plaque and helps to keep her mouth safe from unhealthy germs.
    ISBN 0-8239-5683-0 (lib. bdg. : alk. paper)
    1. Teeth—Care and hygiene—Juvenile literature. 2. Teeth—Juvenile literature. [1.Teeth—Care and hygiene.] I. Title. II. Series.

    RK63 .V64 2000
    617.6'01—dc21   99-049900

Manufactured in the United States of America.

Contents

I brush my teeth every morning and every night. I make sure to keep my teeth very clean.

5

I turn on the water at the sink to wet my toothbrush.

7

My mom helps me squeeze the toothpaste onto my toothbrush. The toothpaste tastes like bubble gum.

9

My mom tells me that brushing helps keep my whole mouth safe from unhealthy germs.

11

I brush my teeth in small, gentle circles. I brush one or two teeth at a time. Brush! Brush!

brush!

brush!

13

My mom tells me we brush our teeth to clean off plaque. Plaque is a coating that covers teeth. Plaque can cause cavities.

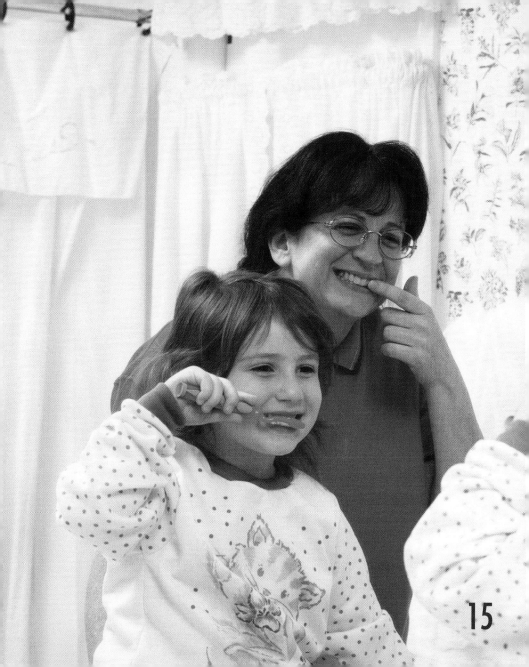

15

I remember to brush my tongue, too. Germs can also live on your tongue.

I fill my cup with water and get ready to rinse my mouth.

19

After I am done brushing I like to smile and look at my clean and healthy teeth!

Words to Know

CUP

SINK

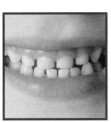
TEETH

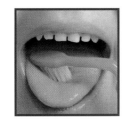
TONGUE

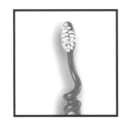
TOOTHBRUSH

TOOTHPASTE

Here are more books to read about brushing your teeth:

Brushing Well
by Helen Frost
Pebble Books

I Know Why I Brush My Teeth
by Kate Rowan
Candlewick Press

To learn more about brushing your teeth, check out these Web sites:
http://www.edoc.co.za/dhw/kidscorner/index.html
http://207.125.132.3/4thgrade/dental.html
http://www.adha.org/kidstuff/index.html
http://www.oralb.com/teaching/lesson/5-8/day1.htm

Index

Word Count: 147

Note to Parents, Teachers, and Librarians

PowerKids Readers are specially designed to get emergent and beginning readers excited about learning to read. Simple stories and concepts are paired with photographs of real kids in real-life situations. Spirited characters and story lines that kids can relate to help readers respond to written language by linking meaning with their own everyday experiences. Sentences are short and simple, employing a basic vocabulary of sight words, as well as new words that describe familiar things and places. Large type, clean design, and photographs corresponding directly to the text all help children to decipher meaning. Features such as a picture glossary and an index help children get the most out of PowerKids Readers. Lists of related books and Web sites encourage kids to explore other sources and to continue the process of learning.

With their engaging stories and vivid photo-illustrations, PowerKids Readers inspire children with the interest and confidence to return to these books again and again. It is this rich and rewarding experience of success with language that gives children the opportunity to develop a love of reading and learning that they will carry with them throughout their lives.